Jonah
The Brat Prophet

Rosilyn Hill

Jonah
The Brat Prophet
Rosilyn Hill, HAS Publishing
Ft. Walton Beach, Fl USA
LCCN 2018934032
ISBN 0-9716805-3-1
Copyright Text and Illustrations 2017 Rosilyn Hill
1st Edition

DEDICATION

This book is dedicated to GOD for the miracle of:
Mason Dewayne Brooks.

ACKNOWLEDGMENTS

Thank you for all those who put up with my requests for help. Thank you anyway if you were not able to help. Some roads we must travel alone. Jonah, The Brat Prophet had to be my journey.

A special thanks To Mrs. Rhoda Adam-Reese, Leonard Mitchell and Corrine Pielli for their editorial assistance. Thanks for giving me poetic license not to be perfect for the sake of rhyme.

Thanks to my illustrators whom will be selected on the final or future versions of Jonah The Brat Prophet.

CHAPTER ONE

FIRST COMMISSION

GOD said to Jonah,

the son of Amit'tai,

saying arise,

go to Nineveh and CRY.

All their wickedness I SEE.

In 40 days destruction shall BE.

Because their evil and

violence are before ME.

JONAH'S FLIGHT

But Jonah rose up to FLEE.

He chose NOT to obey ME.

To Joppa he FLED.

On a ship to Tarshish,

He made a BED.

To do what he wanted

INSTEAD.

THE GREAT STORM

But I, THE LORD sent a great WIND.

The ship started to rock and to BEND.

A mighty tempest the wind caused in the SEA.

To teach Jonah he could NOT flee from ME.

THE MARINERS

The mariners were afraid and CRIED.

Casting their cargo over the SIDE.

Praying every man to

his idol god.

Except for Jonah, who was

taking a NOD.

THE CAPTAIN

The captain, he shouted at Jonah.

O sleeper, fast asleep,

GET THEE UP !!!

Pray to your GOD that

we not PERISH !!!

On our lives HE may think to

CHERISH.

5

CASTING LOTS

The mariners said,

come let us cast lots,

so that we may KNOW.

Who's to blame for this evil, and on them

the guilt will GO.

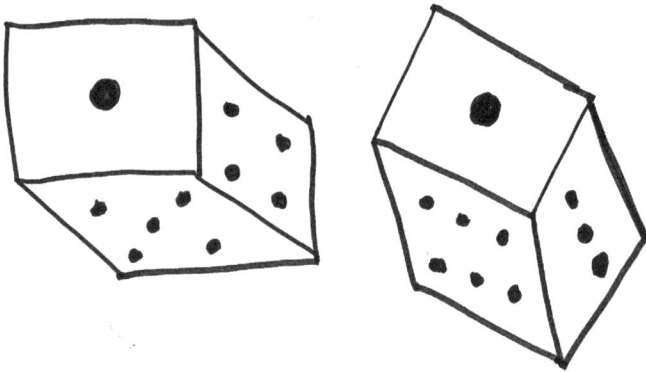

Cast lots   A method used to determine the will of God which were
                 thrown into a small area and then the result was interpreted

THE BLAME

The lot fell on Jonah

He was to BLAME.

The mariners shouted

Questions.

He dropped his head

in SHAME.

THE QUESTIONS

The mariners asked him,

WHY?

WHY?   WHY?

What do you do?

And where does your

country lie?

Where have you come from?

And who are your people?

What must be done to stop this upheaval?

THE REVEAL

Jonah replied, I am a Hebrew,

and I fear THE LORD.

My disobedience has caused

this DISCHORD.

My GOD is THE GOD

of heaven, the sea

and the dry LAND.

Everything and everyone

must obey

HIS COMMAND.

THE SHOCK

The mariners were shocked-struck with awe,

as they began to PLEA.

Tell us what to do right now,

to calm the roaring SEA.

Tell us, tell us quick,

how to end this dreadful STATE.

Tell us, tell us, please before it's too LATE.

THE INSTRUCTIONS

Jonah said, listen carefully.

This is what you must DO.

Obey my instructions exactly,

because what I say will save YOU.

TAKE ME UP-CAST ME FORTH,

over the side of the SHIP.

Then the wind and sea will stop their raging,

so the ship will NOT FLIP.

THE ROARING SEA

YES, throw me into the

deep waters.

YES, throw me into the

raging SEA.

GOD caused the wind and sea

to be angry.

This disaster is

because of ME.

THE MARINERS DISOBEY

NO!   NO!   NO!

cried the mariners.

This we cannot DO.

We see you are a man of GOD.

It would be wrong to harm you.

So they rowed-rowed-rowed the ship.

Trying so hard to reach LAND.

But the mariners soon

discovered that Jonah was right.

You cannot get away from GOD's great HAND.

MARINERS PRAY TO JEHOVAH

The mariners cried,

we beg Thee O LORD,

we beseech Thee.

Please let us NOT die

because of the MAN.

Spare our lives, relieve this strife.

Put NOT his blood on our HANDS.

Then the mariners obeyed

Jonah's instructions.

JONAH CAST OVER

At once the wind and sea ceased from raging.

When they cast Jonah into the DEEP.

NO thunder,

NO lightening,

NO water splashing.

It was so calm, you couldn't hear a PEEP.

THE GREAT FISH

Jonah sank down DEEP.

Where GOD had prepared

a great fish for him to MEET.

THANKSGIVING AND VOWS

The mariners rejoiced.

We thank THEE, O LORD,

We praise THEE.

We now know

how great THOU are.

We here vow our lives

to YOU ever.

There's NO other GOD

but YOU, forever.

THREE DAYS THREE NIGHTS

Meanwhile.

For three days and three NIGHTS,

Jonah thought on his PLIGHT.

He thought on his

disobedient WAYS.

As he remembered

THE LORD,

and sorrow filled his heart;

then he humbled himself and PRAYED.

JONAH'S AFFLICTION

CHAPTER TWO

Jonah said,

My AFFLICTION is my

CONTRADICTION.

As a SERVANT refusing to SERVE.

Now in this darkness

it SMELLS,

in the belly of HELL.

Inside this WHALE,

are like the bars of a JAIL.

JONAH'S PLIGHT

LORD, I am cast from YOUR Sight.

My soul is fainting from FRIGHT.

This water is CHOKING.

The slime on my skin is SMOKING.

I am SINKING and

I am STINKING.

I have seaweeds wrapped

around my HEAD.

My, LORD,

I am almost DEAD.

JONAH'S PRAYER

Jonah continued to cry and pray.

Lying vanity I FORSAKE,

if it is NOT too LATE.

I thought I could run from YOU.

I discovered that was folly, TOO.

LORD, let me pay my VOW.

YOUR servant now knows HOW,

to obey YOUR COMMAND.

Salvation is in YOUR merciful HAND.

JEHOVAH'S ANSWER

GOD, JEHOVAH, heard Jonah prayer and was moved with compassion. Then HE told the fish to release the MAN. The fish obeyed and spit Jonah out on dry LAND.

22

SECOND COMMISSION

CHAPTER THREE

GOD said to Jonah

the second time.

Jonah Jonah,

Arise ! Arise !,

Go ! Go !,   to to

Nineveh ! Nineveh !

That That great great

city city and and

preach preach the the

preaching preaching

that that I I

tell tell you you.

This time Jonah obeyed and went.

<u>JONAH PREACHES</u>

Jonah preached.

In 40 days you all are

going to DIE!

Don't be surprised,

you know WHY !

In 40 days GOD's going

to wipe you OUT !!!

Everyone will

scream and SHOUT.

In 40 days, you die, you're dead,

you are going DOWN.

In 40 days, Nineveh will be overthrown, down
to the GROUND !!!

THE KING'S DECREE

The king made a DECREE.

NO Food, NO Water for ME.

NO throne, NO robe,

NO crown will I WEAR.

By this example, will everyone SHARE.

NINEVAH'S RESPONSE

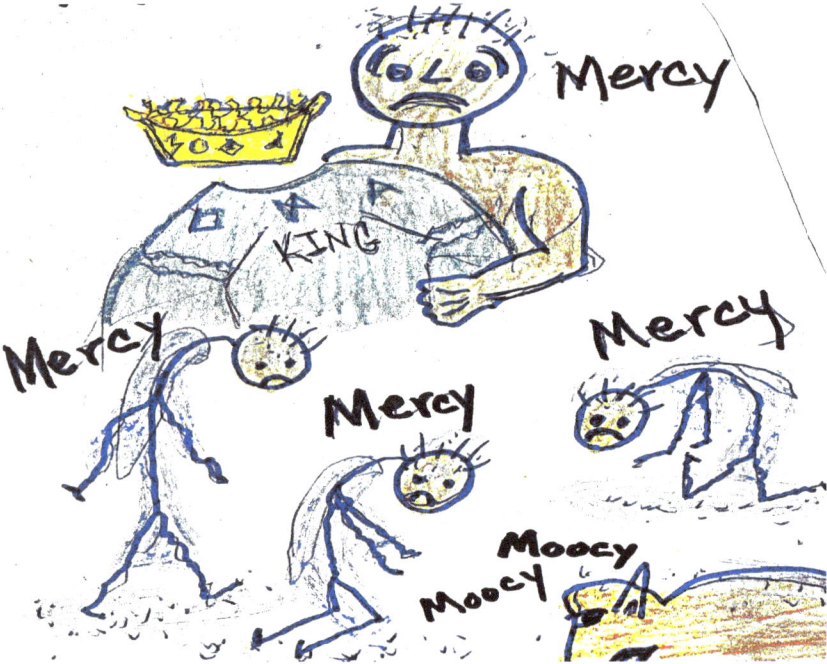

Man and beast,

great and SMALL.

This decree is to ALL.

Sackcloth is our FASHION.

We all will wallow in ASHES.

Everything, everyone to SHARE,

this our destruction we must BARE.

THE KING'S INSTRUCTIONS

The king said, let us cry out

and turn from our EVIL.

Cry, beg, plea for a

REPRIEVEL.

Who knows, maybe GOD

will FORGIVE.

Stop HIS fierce anger

and let us LIVE.

THE PEOPLE'S RESPONSE

The people fasted and prayed.

We will stop and turn from evil. We will stop

our violent way.

From now on, we will do

whatever GOD say.

We promise to love each other,

true to the BONE.

And YOU will be the

only GOD we worship, on the THRONE.

JEHOVAH'S FORGIVENESS

Nineveh believed the

preaching of Jonah.

Nineveh obeyed the

King's DECREE.

GOD took notice

of their repentance.

A stay of execution gave HE.

JONAH'S ANGER

CHAPTER FOUR

God's mercy made Jonah very angry.

He shouted at GOD and he SAID.

I told YOU so, didn't I.

You never wanted them DEAD.

With my own lips,

this is just what I SAID.

While still in my own country,

before I FLED.

O LORD, I want to DIE!

YOU made me a LIE!

For this shame, let me NOT live.

JEHOVAH CONFRONTS JONAH

GOD asked Jonah,

Doest thou well to be angry?

Jonah replied,

YES! Angry to be, well I do.

I knew from the START,

YOU are tender at HEART.

YOU are slow to anger, ever ready to forgive.

YOU are gracious and KIND.

YOUR love is so DIVINE.

Salvation and Mercy are THINE.

JONAH'S DISPLEASURE

So Jonah went out of the city.

He sat on the east side

to SEE.

He made there a booth

to rest in.

Still wanting destruction for

the Hebrews' ENEMY.

THE GOURD

Meanwhile GOD, THE LORD,

prepared HE a GOURD,

for shade over Jonah's head.

To give him RELIEF,

from his terrible GRIEF.

For the gourd, Jonah was

exceedingly glad.

THE WORM

But GOD also prepared a worm.

So when the morning arose

the next DAY.

The worm smote the gourd.

And the gourd, it withered AWAY!

JONAH'S SUFFERING

The sun blazing hot did GLOW.

GOD prepared a vehement

east wind to BLOW.

The sun's heat did beat

upon Jonah's HEAD.

He fainted and wished

he was DEAD.

Then he open his mouth to CRY.

It is better NOT to live.

Let me DIE !!!

JEHOVAH CONFRONTS JONAH AGAIN

GOD asked Jonah,

Doest thou well to be angry?

YES, angry to be, well I DO!

On our enemies, YOU did show mercy.

But my little gourd YOU SLEW.

GOD said to Jonah,

You want to die,

that is SILLY.

For the gourd you

did NOT do DIDDLY.

Diddly   To do nothing or very little for, pretty little; zero

JONAH'S LESSONS

Listen to ME my son, let ME teach you.

I love you, I AM LOVE,

this you already KNOW.

In that great city of Nineveh, there are
120,000 persons or SO.

They cannot tell their right hand from their
left HAND.

There is also much cattle in that LAND.

When they heeded MY

warning and REPENTED.

MY LOVE and MERCY

could then take a STAND.

Judgment and Destruction RELENTED.
Amazing Grace became MY PLAN.

JONAH MOVES ON

Now gather yourself my young servant.

You still have work to do for ME.

Your deeds will all be recorded

and go down into HISTORY.

As long as time continues.

The story of Jonah

will be TOLD.

All will know, I THE LORD, do offer,

SALVATION as MY ultimate GOAL.

THE END

Jonah,The Brat Prophet
Rosilyn Hill, HAS Publishing
Ft. Walton Beach, Fl USA
LCCN 2018934032
ISBN 0-9716805-3-1
Copyright Text and Illustrations 2017 Rosilyn Hill
1st Edition